Yorkshire Scene

by

Ronald Willis

Photography by Thelma Willis

Published by Hendon Publishing Company Limited, Hendon Mill, Nelson, Lancashire.
Text & Photographs © Ronald & Thelma Willis, 1977
Printed by Fretwell & Brian Ltd., Howden Hall, Silsden, Keighley, Yorks.

TWO YORK TOWERS

At a point in the Museum Gardens, York, where the modern and Roman ground levels are almost the same, the western tower of the fourth-century legionary fortress still stands above ground. Its counterpart in the south angle was found in Feasegate in the heart of the city's shopping centre in 1832 and was further examined in 1852 and 1956. The plan is the same in outline as the west angle tower and the wall stands to a height of nine feet under commercial premises. A tentative plan to make the tower available to the public was abandoned some years ago. The south tower's present position, about ten feet below street level, shows that the river front in Roman times had a marked slope in this direction.

This dramatic survivor of the Roman defences has been known since the late-seventeenth century as the Multangular Tower, as it has nine faces, but was called Ellerendyng or Elrondyng in the Middle ages. The tower is surmounted by late-thirteenth century walls up to two feet thick, the stone blocks being markedly

Left: The western angle tower of the fourth-century legionary fortress at York (Eboracum) the small masonry blocks contrasting with the larger stones of the late-thirteenth-century walls which surmount it. Known as the Multangular Tower, it stands today in the city's Museum Gardens.

larger than the Roman. Until cleared by the Yorkshire Philosophical Society in 1831, the interior was filled with earth up to the beginning of the medieval walls.

A short way to the north-east, behind the public library, is the excavated Anglian Tower, perhaps of seventh-century date. It may have been used for only a short period before being buried beneath a rampart in about the year 900. It was opened in the thirteenth-century and was not re-discovered until 1839 when it was broken into by workmen making a tunnel between a house in St. Leonard's Place and stables in what was then known as Mint Yard.

ENIGMA OF THE CONEY STREET 'ADMIRAL'.

One of the country's most attractive public clocks is the hallmark of a city church—St. Martin-le-Grand—which passed through the fire-bomb Baedeker raid of April 1942 to serve today, in a changed form, as an oasis of quiet in busy Coney Street, York.

The re-designed church was opened in April 1968 as a chapel of ease and garden of rest. Its great clock, hanging at right angles over the street on an elaborate bracket of swirling ironwork, is topped by the wooden figure of an eighteenth-century naval officer taking an observation of the sun with a simple cross-staff. The clock was added to the church in 1668 but the 'Little

Admiral', as the figure is known, dates from just over a century later. He was a badly charred victim of the raid and did not return to his position until May 1966.

Despite its familiar title, the figure appears to wear a Royal Navy captain's undress uniform in use during the years 1774-87, which ties in with the suggestion that it was added to the clock during the renovations of 1778-79. The preserved parish accounts make no mention of the figure during those years, though there is a reference to 'ornaments'.

What was its origin? Was it made specially for the clock or was it an adaptation? I believe the answer lies in the fourth chapter of Dickens's Dombey And Son where he gives a detailed description of shops and offices surrounding the family firm in the City of London. He mentions 'little timber midshipmen in obsolete naval uniforms' outside the shops of nautical instrument-makers. They had probably been there for the past fifty or sixty years. Singling out one of these figures, Dickens said it had the right leg forward and was wearing shoe buckles and a flapped waistcoat. Except for the question of rank, this is a pretty close description of the 'admiral' of Coney Street. Perhaps he started life as an eighteenth-century trade sign.

A GASLIGHT MEMORY

For many years a tobacconist's, and now occupied by an antique dealer, a small shop in Low Petergate, York, retains a curious link with its recent past. Attached to the left-hand side of the door, and unnoticed by most passers-by, is a metal horse's head. In past days its nostrils flared with gas-jets, offering an instant light to the passing smoker. Not long ago, it was re-gilded by the York Civic Trust.

Gaslight first came into the lives of York citizens on the night of Monday, March 22, 1824. There were crowds in the streets, the Minster bells rang and all three local newspapers were enthusiastic about the "new era of light in old Ebor". They contrasted the glitter of the gas with the "dim and murky glare" of the infrequent oil-lamps it had replaced.

The Courant reported that "the large lamp in the Pavement had a very good effect. The fitting up of the light in the several shops is very splendid, and the large circular light over the door of Mr. Barber, at the Black Swan, was generally admired." The Chronicle had a look at the Theatre Royal which was "brilliantly illuminated, the saloon, lobbies and front of the boxes being hung with elegant chandeliers lighted with gas." The Gazette found that "the streets for several hours presented the appearance of a fair, so eager were the inhabitants to witness the novel spectacle.."

Throughout the seventeenth and eighteenth centuries there had been experiments with coal gas for lighting,

but it was not until 1798 that it was put to serious use at the Boulton and Watt foundry in Birmingham. Gas first lit London streets in 1807.

SIGNS OF THE TIMES

High up on the facade of this same shop stands one of the city's rare trade signs—a wooden Indian of the "cigar store" type, made at the turn of the eighteenth and nineteenth centuries. Though no longer serving its original purpose, it has been allowed to stay on its bracket over the street as a colourful survivor of the days when such signs were to be seen everywhere.

Many of the city's old signs have found a new home in the York Castle Museum, and include a huge padlock which used to advertise a hardware shop in Parliament Street; a large broomhead from a Petergate brush shop; a clogger's sign; a long whip which identified the saddler's shop which used to stand on the corner of St. Saviourgate; a goldbeater's sign in the form of a gilded hand holding a hammer; a large glass jar over the glass shop in the Museum's Kirkgate; and an outsize riding boot which hung outside a shoemaker's shop.

Left: In the past the nostrils of this small metal horse's head, attached to the doorway of a former tobacconist's shop in Low Petergate, York, flared with gas-jets, offering a light to any passing smoker.

5

Then there are the two Scottish Highlanders and an Indian outside the Kirkgate tobacconist's shop; a barber's pole with bleeding-bowl attached; an apothecary's pestle and mortar; a bunch of grapes hanging from the painted signboard of the "Windmill Inn"; a hanging sign of the Sun Insurance Company outside the Fire Station; a large gun over the gunsmith's shop; a pawnbroker's sign in "Alderman's Walk"; and a ten-gallon blue and white patterned jug over the china shop.

STOCKS AND TOMBSTONE AT A HAUNTED CHURCH

Holy Trinity Church in Micklegate, York, a fragment of a once great Benedictine priory, is perhaps unique in stating on its notice-board that the building was haunted in the nineteenth century. The historian Baring Gould in his Yorkshire Oddities recorded accounts from eye-witnesses who claimed to have seen a woman, sometimes accompanied by a second woman and child, crossing the east window during daytime services. Movement of trees in the churchyard was thought to be causing an illusion, and they were cut down. The woman still appeared. However, since the chancel was built in 1886 there have been no further reports.

The twelfth-century nave pillars of the church belonged to a conventual church which was half as long again and much higher than the present one. Records mention a chapter house and cloisters. Dormitories, refectory, infirmary, brewhouse, stables and all the other domestic buildings must have stood on land now covered by modern buildings to the south and west. The gatehouse, which fronted on to Micklegate with an attractive archway, was destroyed as late as 1855 for the building of Priory Street. The priory was surrendered during the Dissolution in December 1538 and for the next couple of generations the site was robbed of its valuable dressed stone. The central tower collapsed during a storm on February 5, 1551, and the church was demolished in stages. The Norman doorway now in the centre of Sir Arthur Ingram's almshouses in Bootham (now converted into flats) was bought and installed there for 13s 4d.

The church contains a wall monument to Dr. John Burton who died in 1771. Referred to in Laurence Sterne's Tristram Shandy as Dr. Slop, he was a Jacobite antiquary imprisoned after the 1745 Rebellion. He remained a close friend of Flora Macdonald.

The churchyard offers a strange set of stocks with only five holes. There appears to be no solution on record. The five holes could have been cut to accommodate two whole persons and a one-legged offender, but perhaps a more likely explanation is that at some time in the unremembered past the old stocks were in process of being sawn up for firewood. A public-spirited antiquarian stopped the desecration, but not before one end—the end containing the sixth hole—had been lopped off.

A small, defaced monument near the vestry door is a reminder of the evening of Saturday, October 15, 1768 when the London to York stagecoach was travelling along The Mount towards Micklegate Bar. When the driver attempted to overtake another vehicle, the coach overturned and a nineteen-year-old passenger sitting on the box was killed. He never reached his home in Morpeth, Northumberland.

WATER FROM A "WAYSIDE SHRINE"

Standing in Museum Street, York, near the entrance to the Museum Gardens, a small stone structure flourishes its curling crockets and leafy capitals. It could almost be mistaken for a medieval wayside shrine, but the date 1880 in stonemason's gothic, the carved dolphins and the brass lion mask identify it as a Victorian drinking fountain. A press of the button brought a jet of water from the lion's mouth, to fall into the waiting basin supported by a short but elaborate pillar.

Right: This handsome stone drinking fountain of 1880, carved by a local sculptor, stands in Museum Street, York, looking like a medieval wayside shrine.

It was given to the city by a Mr. Henry Cowling and made by the York sculptor Job Cole who shared his Gillygate premises with a builder and a marine store dealer.

The question of public drinking fountains had been raised at a York City Council meeting as far back as January 1859 when a councillor said that "easy access to a continuous supply of good drinking water has been found to promote the comfort of the working classes and to be favourable to good moral habits." An alderman added his weight by saying that the amenity would be "of advantage to working men, promote their morality and be the means of perhaps keeping them out of public houses in the summer season."

ROMAN COLUMN

The centre point of the Roman legionary fortress at York is today occupied by the Minster, which lies on a line diagonal to that of the fortress. This position was held by the principia or headquarters building which at one time included a great hall larger than the Minster's nave. Parallel with the £2,000,000 Minster restoration scheme of 1967-72 ran a full-scale archaeological investigation, during which three column bases from the Roman hall, each weighing five tons, were found exactly where predicted. The width of the nave between the columns was 40ft. and the building, erected about AD 108 during the administration of Trajan, was 50 ft. high. Towards the end of the restoration scheme a fourth-century pillar, found in pieces under the south transept, was re-erected by the York Civic Trust outside the Minster's south door to commemorate the 1900th anniversary of the city's founding.

During the archaeological investigation, when some 24,000 flashbulbs were used to photograph the finds, it was discovered that in the seventh century the buildings on this site were not of contemporary construction, for the great military headquarters and adjacent buildings still stood and were to remain standing for a further two centuries.

THE SIGN OF MINERVA IN "BOOKBINDERS' ALLEY"

The goddess of wisdom occupies a prime site in the centre of York, at the junction of one of the city's busiest pedestrian junctions and overlooking the line of the Romans' via principalis. The figure of Minerva, with her books and attendant owl, is a charming

Right: A fourth-century pillar from the headquarters building of the Roman legionary fortress, discovered in pieces under the south transept of York Minster during restoration work, was erected on a site outside the South Door.

feature to be found at the corner of Minster Gates, one of York's earliest 'foot-streets', which appears on nineteenth-century maps as South Entrance and was known 200 years ago as Bookbinders' Alley. The fact that this group has survived, not in a museum, but as part of the city's fabric, is just one instance of York's capacity to surprise and delight.

There seems little doubt that the figure was made specifically for this site, and it is probably the work of Francis Wolstenholme, a member of a family of craftsmen whose house still stands at the corner of Bootham and Gillygate. The house, now Nos. 3 and 5 Gillygate, was built by his brother Thomas in the late eighteenth century. Thomas was a joiner, carver and maker of composition ornaments. Francis succeeded to the business after Thomas's death in 1812. After the Minster fire of 1829, which was started by the deranged Jonathan Martin and destroyed the medieval choir and lady chapel, the Wolstenholmes, then operating from the King's Manor, played an important part in the £55,000 restoration scheme.

Minster Gates, a short, paved street leading to the south door of the Minster, was connected with the book trade in 1645 when Francis Mawburne took up his freedom of the city on payment of £6 13s 4d. Throughout the eighteenth century the street was a fashionable meeting ground for authors and book-lovers. William Tesseyman occupied the Sign of the Crown there in 1760 and in 1772 was one of the publishers of The English Garden by William Mason, a Precentor of the Minster. Tesseyman's advertisements in eighteenth-century newspapers show that he was a versatile trader, selling novels and rat poison side by side.

MOSAIC FLOORS

Of all the Roman mosaic floors, whole or fragmentary, which have been uncovered in York, that of the Four Seasons has the most immediate appeal. The seasons appear as heads in each corner, together with an appropriate symbol . . . the hay-rake of summer, the bird of spring, the grapes of autumn and the bare branch of winter. The central head of Medusa is damaged.

The floor first came to light in 1853 while a local builder was digging a drain in Toft Green, and had probably belonged to a house of the fourth century with at least five rooms and three decorative floors. It was in the best part of the civil town—the colonia—and may have become a treasured "period" property in its time. Today, with other fragments, the surviving floor may be seen in the Yorkshire Museum.

In the past a number of other floors under the modern city have been discovered, and sometimes lost again. In the summer of 1976 a geometric mosaic floor, first found in 1851, was "re-discovered" and lifted for preservation.

In 1814 a Roman tessellated pavement was found under the Jolly Bacchus public house near Micklegate Bar, but it was ruined by unchecked souvenir hunters. Fragments were removed by the Corporation in 1837, but what was left probably still lies under the city wall. The inn was taken down in 1873. A coloured engraving of the pavement was published not long after the discovery. It showed various types of border enclosing a central octagonal panel decorated with two stags. Joints of venison filled the corner panels.

A building with pavement was found in 1871 under "the buttress on the left side of the entrance door of the church of St. Mary Castlegate." Nothing more is known.

Building debris found in 1874 on the approaches to Scarborough Bridge, north of York Station, included painted wall plaster and a large fragment of tessellated pavement. A building with tessellated pavement was found in 1813 during the making of a sunken fence near Clifton Grove, later St. Olave's School. A similar find was made in the nineteenth century behind Acomb House in Front Street.

MEMORIES OF A VANISHED CHURCH

A lofty medieval church with a handsome cupola-topped seventeenth-century tower once stood on the corner of Pavement and The Shambles in York. It was demolished in the eighties of the last century and we must rely on engravings and old photographs for some idea of its appearance, though a finely detailed picture of the interior was painted in 1884 by a York architect and is now in private possession.

Today the church of St. Crux is represented on the site by the small parish room built from the materials, a building which is much photographed by tourists, for a plaque explaining the origin of Whip-Ma-Whop-Ma-Gate, the city's shortest street, is fixed to the east wall.

Though a church of this name was held by the Count of Mortain in 1087, old St. Crux was probably built in the fifteenth century. By the 1880's the building was in poor condition. It was partly taken down in 1884, but re-building never began and it remained a ruin in the city centre until cleared away in 1887. The parish, which covered a small area round the church and ran south-eastwards to the River Foss, was united with All Saints', Pavement.

Some of the better monuments were preserved in the parish room, the largest being that of Sir Robert Watter, his wife and three children. Margaret Watter died in 1608 and her husband in 1612. Twice Lord Mayor of York, Sir Robert presented the city with the gold chain of office for the first citizen, founded a charity hospital near Fishergate Postern and built the now demolished Haberdashers' Hall on the corner of Walmgate and George Street.

The south-east corner of the room is occupied by the wall monument to Sir Tancred Robinson, a naval flag officer who died in 1754 and was, like Watter, twice Lord Mayor of York.

Books form an appropriate decoration on the tablet to Roger Bellwood, "Sergeant-at-Law, a learned man, much experienced in Law and Equity especially", who died in 1694. His books are shown with the spines reversed, like those on the monument to Archbishop Accepted Frewen in the Minster.

A NINETEENTH-CENTURY OBSERVATORY

The distinctive little building in the heart of the Museum Gardens at York was built as an astronomical observatory in 1832. An eminent architect once said that the shape and proportions of the stonework were so reminiscent of the Tower of the Four Winds in Athens that the designer may have been inspired by it. It has also been said that its conical roof began life as the roof of a summer-house in the rectory garden at South Kilworth, Leicestershire, the home of Dr. Pearson who, in the reign of William IV, was vice-president of the Royal Astronomical Society.
It is to Dr. Pearson that the observatory owes its ex-istence. When the British Association held its original meeting in York in 1831 Dr. Pearson promised the Yorkshire Philosophical Society that if they would build an observatory he would present them with two of the best instruments in his possession. The observatory was built and the instruments installed—an equatorially-mounted telescope of 4 in. aperture and a transit instrument. Dr. Pearson also added a sidereal clock by Barraud and the conical revolving roof.

In 1858 a comet was observed from the building during its passage in late September, and on August 21, 1867, a small party watched three of Jupiter's satellites cross the disc.

In 1977 the future of the building was under discussion.

ROMAN BATH

The presence of a large bath-house in the forepart of the Roman legionary fortress at York is unusual, and today its remains form one of the visible links with the Roman past, as they are preserved in the basement of a public house in St. Sampson's Square. In 1971 the brewers changed the name of the pub from the Mail

Right: A small-scale version of Bramhope railway tunnel is to be seen in the graveyard of Otley parish church as a memorial to the men who died during its construction between 1845 and 1849.

Coach Inn to The Roman Bath, and had a circular viewing panel cut in the floor of the lounge so that patrons may admire the illuminated bath. The bath-house was built early in the fourth century after the demolition of other military buildings, and so dates from the time when the south-west defences of the fortress were extensively altered.

The bath was first excavated in 1930-31, and the remains were found to consist of the east corner of the south-east side of the frigidarium, containing a cold plunge bath, and a large part, including an apse, of a heated room, the caldarium. The cold bath, which had a 4 in. outlet hole, had a floor of tiles embedded in concrete spread on cobbles resting on natural clay, and its sides were revetted with coursed tiles. One tile had the stamp of the Sixth Legion. The bath had been deliberately filled in with large blocks of sandstone.

In 1972 came the dramatic discovery of a major Roman sewer running under this part of the city centre. Contractors working on a development site in the Swine-gate-Church Street area lifted a large stone slab at some depth below cellar floor level and found an extensive culvert. Archaeologists identified it as a Roman sewer and time was allowed for a full investigation.

From the entry point, the sewer ran for about 15 ft, in a south-easterly direction under Church Street and about 150 ft. in a north-westerly direction towards Stone-gate, where it ended in a Roman wall of dressed stone. About 12 ft. along the north-west stretch was a junction chamber about 6 ft. high where the culvert veered off under Swinegate towards a presumed bath complex. Remains of beetles in the silt gave a clue to the uses to which the sewer and its channels had been put. Three intaglio stones were found in the sewer, one a figure with shield and spear, the second a profile head and the third a figure mounted on a horse.

The sewer probably dates from the re-planning of the fortress in the second century. There are few such systems in northern Europe in which one can walk for any distance.

HISTORY BELOW GROUND

One of the most unusual "history trails" in the country lies beneath York Minster in an underground area which did not exist before the five-year restoration scheme. The new Undercroft was created in the large void left by the removal of thousands of tons of soil and rubble and their replacement by compact concrete foundations. The space was turned into a linked series of 12 ft. high rooms capped by a modern, deeply coffered ceiling. But the steps which lead down from the south transept are not just a route to the past. The designers of the Undercroft have reminded visitors of the reason for its existence by allowing the concrete foundations and the huge polished steel nuts retaining the reinforcing stress rods to be seen without any attempt to disguise their purpose.

In the south-western area of the Undercroft may be seen something of the Roman fortress at a point 12 ft. 6 in. below the present floor level of the south aisle of the nave. In this chamber is a piece of the north-east wall of the second-century cross-hall of the legionary headquarters. Roman paintings in their restored form are displayed near the remains of the office wall they once covered. The artist's pastel colours were preserved intact through the sixteen centuries which passed between the day they were applied to the plastered wall and the moment of their discovery. The scenes include dove-like birds, painted pillars, panels in imitation of marble, a theatrical mask of tragedy and an enigmatic robed figure.

The Treasury, reached by a flight of steps from the area under the central tower and not far below the floor of the choir, has as its centrepiece a display case given by the Goldsmiths' Company. On permanent exhibition is the life's work of a York citizen, William Lee, who made a priceless collection of York silver dating from 1475 to 1858.

A painted replica of the coffin lid of the thirteenth-century Archbishop Walter de Gray is a reminder of a dramatic discovery in January 1968 when the archbishop's tomb, in the south transept, was restored.

When workmen lifted off the effigy and canopy they revealed a colour painting on the stone coffin lid almost as fresh as the day it was sealed. A full-length portrait of de Gray, it had remained airtight for more than 700 years. Colouring from the painting had been drawn into the mortar of the canopy foundation to give a "fresco" transfer. On the night of May 3, 1968, within two days of the 713th anniversary of the archbishop's death, the tomb was opened in the presence of a select circle of experts. The coffin contained an ivory-topped crozier, a jewelled ring and a silver-gilt chalice. These objects were removed for display in the Treasury, but the bones were not disturbed.

MEDIEVAL COUNTRYMEN AT WORK

The rattle of coffee cups to be heard in the courtyard of St. William's College whose half-timbered frontage is such a feature of College Street, York, is an indication of how this fifteenth-century building is keeping up with the times. In July 1976 a new restaurant—St. William's Refectory—was opened primarily for Minster visitors, though open to anyone from Monday to Saturday. This was a joint venture between the Minster Dean and Chapter and a catering firm which also runs a restaurant in the Undercroft of Durham Cathedral.

Built for the Minster's chantry priests in the 1460's the college passed through a number of hands after the Reformation and finally became tenements which

were, as an old photograph shows, pretty far down the social scale. At the turn of this century it was restored and used for meetings by the Convocation of York until the amalgamation of the Convovations of Canterbury and York into the Synod of the Church of England. In the middle of the seventeenth century it entered on a few months of glory when, in March 1642, Charles I moved his court to York. The press of the King's printer was set up in the college and it was from this building that Charles' proclamation was issued, announcing his intention of raising his standard at Nottingham.

Few visitors to this fascinating building notice that on curved brackets, each about 2 ft. high, under the over-hanging storey of the inner courtyard are nine carved wooden figures which open a window on fifteenth-century life. They form an almost complete set of the months of the year. It has been suggested that the month of January is missing, making the carving of a man warming himself over a fire the February figure. It is to be seen directly over the inner doorway leading from the street.

Using this as a basis, March is a man pruning trees, April a woman with a hawk on her wrist (or possibly holding a bunch of flowers), June is a mower, August a man reaping corn with a sickle, September a boy

Left: Protected by the porch of St. Gregory's Minster, Kirkdale, is a remarkable Saxon sundial.

gathering grapes and October the beating of oaks for acorns. The remaining two figures cannot be identified.

DICK TURPIN'S EXECUTION

Though the term "topsman" has a curiously modern ring it was, in fact, an eighteenth-century euphemism for "hangman". Use of it was made in a contemporary newspaper account of Dick Turpin's execution at the York Tyburn on Saturday, April 7, 1739, when, with horse stealer John Stead, he stepped off the ladder into space, behaving "with the greatest assurance to the very last."

"It was very remarkable," commented the York Courant on April 10, "that as he mounted the ladder his right leg trembled; on which he stampt it down with an air, and with undaunted courage look'd round about him, and after speaking a few words to the Topsman, he threw himself off the ladder and expired in about five minutes. Before his death he declared himself to be the notorious highwayman, Turpin, and confessed to the Topsman a great number of robberies which he had committed."

A full report of the trial was published on Tuesday, April 10, 1739. Its basis was the note taken by Mr. Thomas Kyll, "professor of shorthand", who was in court when Turpin appeared before Sir William Chapple on March 22. Printed by Ward and Chandler and sold at sixpence in their shop near Temple Bar, London, and in Coney Street, York, the report included a letter Turpin received from his father while under sentence of death.

Turpin's popularity with the mob was demonstrated after the execution. The body was taken to the Blue Boar, an inn in Castlegate, and next morning was buried in St. George's churchyard. The following day "resurrection men" took up the corpse and hid it in the garden of a York surgeon's house. Determined that the highwayman's body should not be used for dissection, the mob discovered it, carried it through the streets, replaced it in the coffin, covered it with unslaked lime and re-buried it in the grave. The inscription on the modern headstone in a green plot in George Street begins: "John Palmer otherwise Richard Turpin . . ."

MONUMENT TO THE TUNNELLERS

So many died in the building of the £500,000, 3,763-yard Bramhope Tunnel on the Leeds-Thirsk line between 1845 and 1849, that the contractor, James Bray, an iron and brass founder of Black Bull Street, Leeds, felt obliged to erect a memorial to them, partly at his own expense.

His model to the victims is a small-scale version of the tunnel's northern entrance, which was built in castellated style, with towers, arrow slits and battlements framing the tunnel mouth. Today it is one of the more unusual sights of the market town of Otley, standing in a cut-off section of the parish church's graveyard.

When work started in the autumn of 1845, Bramhope was invaded by 2,300 quarrymen, masons, labourers, tunnel men, excavators and carpenters—and, of course, their wives and children. The company housed the work force in 350 wooden huts known as "bothies" and granted £100 to the village school where classes increased ninefold. The workings were often water-logged and more than 1,500 million gallons had to be pumped away. No-one bothered to keep a record of the accidents until 1847, but it is known that there was a regular sprung cart service to the new Leeds Infirmary.

The first train carried the local Temperance Band with shareholders, passing through stations decorated with banners and boughs of oak and ash. Lunch in the Thirsk carriage shed included meat sandwiches, prime Cheshire cheese, bread and confectionery. A temporary bar served ale, porter and spirits. First class fare from Leeds to Thirsk was nine shillings, giving the passenger the luxury of a bench padded with horsehair, leather armrests and a sheepskin rug. Second class was a little more spartan, and third class offered standing room only in the early days. Later, benches with wrought iron armrests were provided.

A SAXON SUNDIAL

Isolated in a deeply wooded valley between Ryedale and the high moors, St. Gregory's Minster is a building of the mid-eleventh century. Helping to date the church is its most remarkable feature, to be seen over the south door under the protection of the porch. It is a Saxon sundial with an inscription.

Its fine state of preservation is due to its being hidden under a coat of plaster until discovered in 1771, and from then on to the shelter given by the porch. It would appear to be in its original position and consists of a stone slab, seven feet long, divided into three sections. The centre one is the dial, while the outer ones contain the inscription, recording the re-building of the church. The translated words above the dial read: "This is day's sun marker at every time."

A modern version of the remaining inscription says: "Orm Gamal's son bought St. Gregory's Minster when it was all broken down and fallen and he let it be made anew from the ground to Christ and to St. Gregory in the days of Edward the King and of Tosti the Earl. And Haward me wrought and Brand Priests."

RYEDALE FOLK MUSEUM

The rag rug, homely mantel ornaments, black-leaded range and—in due season—pots of wild flowers on the broad window-sills, make the visitor to the thatched cottage in the Ryedale Folk Museum at Hutton-le-Hole feel like a time traveller. Sitting in the kitchen's Windsor chair, one finds it hard to believe that the cottage was dismantled in 1972 and transported stone by stone from Harome, near Helmsley.

This cottage, once known as Prospect House, is only one of a number of traditional buildings re-erected on the museum's open-air site in the heart of the village which lies in the North York Moors National Park. The Cruck House stood for nearly 500 years in Stangend, Danby, before its demolition and reconstruction. The Manor House, also from Harome, was lived in from 1600 to 1950 when it became a storehouse.

A remarkable feature of the Cruck House, a typical yeoman's dwelling, is the post which supports the crossbeam of the smoke-hood which overhangs the open hearth. Known as a witch post, it carries carvings which were believed to act as a talisman against witchcraft.

A reconstructed glass furnace in the grounds is the only substantial example in the country of the type of furnace introduced into Britain during the reign of Elizabeth I by French and Flemish glassworkers.

In the 200-year-old farm buildings fronting the village's

main street is housed the museum's collection of smaller exhibits illustrating rural life in the area up to comparatively recent times, including old photographs and craft tools.

SHIP AND SWASTIKA

Exposed to everything the English climate can throw at it, the remarkable south door of the church of St. Helen in Stillingfleet may be 800 years old, contemporary with the twelfth-century building. In countries less blasé about ancient inheritance, it would probably be kept under armoured glass.

Just to see the ironwork on its pitted face is worth a long journey, and indeed it draws visitors from all parts of the world. First, there are two huge 'C'-shaped hinges ending in serpents' or dragons' heads, then a long, plaited, chain-like strip. In the top left-hand corner are two rather vulnerable human figures and a complicated swastika. But all the magical power of this door is concentrated in the ship which appears on the right. About a century ago, some learned authority thought it represented Noah's Ark, but there is no doubt in my mind that it is a Scandinavian longship with a long steering oar.

Right: The homely farmhouse interior to be found at the thatched cottage from Harome which was dismantled and re-constructed in the Ryedale Folk Museum, Hutton-le-Hole.

AN ARCHBISHOP'S CASTLE

The great castle of the Archbishop of York which stood in the riverside village of Cawood, was demolished in 1646 and some of the stones were taken by water to Bishopthorpe, upstream towards York, to be used in extensions to the Palace there. In 1783 the vaults and foundations were dug up, but for some fortunate reason the graceful fifteenth-century gatehouse was allowed to stay, a solid stone reminder of past splendours.

Seven Archbishops of York died here, Henry VIII and his young bride Catherine Howard stayed in the castle and in 1572 it was one of the many resting places of Elizabeth I during her progress through the country. But perhaps its most famous connection was with Cardinal Wolsey towards the end of his life. Out of favour with the king and left with nothing but the See of York, he came to Cawood hoping for a little peace. He arrived after Michaelmas 1530 and made a start on restoration work. He was to have been enthroned Archbishop of York on the Monday of All Hallows, November 7, but on the preceding Friday was arrested on a charge of high treason by the Earl of Northumberland. He died on the last day of the month at Leicester Abbey.

If the records are to be believed, Cawood Castle was the scene in the mid-fifteenth century of a gargantuan banquet to celebrate the elevation of George Neville, brother of Warwick the Kingmaker, to the archbishopric. Two thousand cooks, 500 kitcheners, 500 scullions, and 1,000 waiters prepared and served 500 deer, six wild bulls, a dozen seals and prime porpoises, 300 oxen, 2,000 pigs and calves, 5,000 rabbits, 8,000 chickens, 4,000 geese, 800 swans, 400 cranes, 400 curlews, 400 peacocks, 400 dishes of jelly, 500 custards, 5,000 hot pasties, 300 tuns of ale and 100 tuns of wine.

A GREEK 'ADVENTURE'

A simple monument in York Minster's south choir aisle and a lavishly decorated country church near Ripon are drawn together by a single thread . . . the lonely road from Athens to Marathon.

Both monument and church were erected in memory of Frederick Vyner, murdered by Greek brigands in the spring of 1870. His mother, Lady Mary Vyner, had the church built in the park of her home, Newby Hall at Skelton between Boroughbridge and Ripon, choosing as architect William Burges, who also designed not only the astonishingly rich church at Studley Royal but the riotous Cardiff Castle and the toytown towers of Castell Coch in the deep beechwoods overlooking the River Taff.

Standing at the end of a dark tunnel of clipped yews, the Church of Christ the Consoler is lit by exceptionally beautiful Victorian glass. No crude colours here, but swimming motes of the gentlest orange and misty grape blue, touching the delicate features of the carved angels, leaning forward from the shadows of the high organ case with their cymbals and tambourine. Outside, at the east end, an odd pair of heraldic beasts act as finials. They appear to be seated dogs wearing helmets which sprout the Vyner crest—a bent right arm, mailed and holding a six-pointed spur.

This elaborate and tragic shrine looks back to the morning of April 11, 1870, when a small party set off from Athens on a sight-seeing jaunt. The party included Lord and Lady Muncaster; a Mr. Herbert, secretary to the English Legation; Count de Boyl, second secretary to the Italian Legation, with his servant; a Mr. and Mrs. Lloyd and their daughter; and Frederick Vyner. That spring, bandits had crossed the border from Turkey and were reported to be at large in the northern provinces of Greece. The party asked for protection on their trip, and two mounted policemen accompanied them.

Because the road to Marathon was particularly desolate, the government ordered an infantry detachment to patrol the route in pairs. The party's two carriages were escorted into Marathon by sixteen armed men. It was in the evening, on their return, that a foolish decision was made. Keen to reach Athens as soon as possible, someone in the party urged the carriages to put on speed so that although the mounted police kept pace, the foot soldiers were soon left behind. As the party reached Macro Narappos Bridge shots were fired and the police fell wounded. The carriages were stopped and surrounded by bandits who took the passengers some distance from the road in spite of fire from the soldiers who had by now caught up—but too late to be of any use.

In an unexpectedly chivalrous mood, the bandits decided to send the women back to Athens in the carriages, and suggested that the men should draw lots to decide who should walk into Athens to arrange a £50,000 ransom. This duty fell to Frederick Vyner who immediately handed it over to Lord Muncaster whose life, he said, was more valuable than his own. But the bandits wanted more than money; they also demanded an amnesty from the Greek government for all the offences they had committed.

Through an intermediary the government argued with the bandits for several days. In an attempt to persuade the gang into a more reasonable frame of mind, it was decided to send a party of soldiers into the area with orders not to fire or use violence. But, as often happens in such situations, firing did break out and the bandits moved the prisoners to a safer spot in the mountains. Excitement, fatigue and the bad food they had been obliged to eat began to tell, and as they dropped in their tracks, one by one, in the rough country, they were shot. Later their bodies were found and a funeral service was held in Athens cathedral. Members of the gang were afterwards captured, tried and executed.

A "KNEELING" CROSS

The fifteenth-century church of All Saints in the neatly by-passed village of Ripley, near Ripon, has two curious external features. In the churchyard on the north side is a 5 ft. high pedestal made from two blocks of stone of unequal size. In the centre of the smaller, upper block is a rectangular hole which originally held the shaft of a large cross. Around the lower block have been cut deep niches intended for kneeling in, although they are so narrow that this could only have been done with some difficulty. This cross, anything from 600 to 800 years old, is rare, if not unique.

A sad reminder of the Civil War of the seventeenth century are marks on the external east wall of the church, made by the bullets fired by Cromwellian soldiers when they executed loyalist prisoners after the Battle of Marston Moor, near York, in 1644. When the church was re-pointed, a number of flattened lead bullets were found embedded in the wall.

The church is just a step from historic Ripley Castle, home of the Ingilbys, whose crest, a boar's head tusked and with a flower in its mouth, may be seen among the ironwork trappings of the gates The Ingilby wild boar is also to be seen in a corner of the village's cobbled square where it surmounts a drinking fountain of 1907, provided by a member of the family who have lived here since the middle of the fourteenth century.

AN OLD SOLDIER OF THE NAPOLEONIC WARS

Matthew Grimes was among Napoleon's escort on board the Bellerophon during the voyage to St. Helena. He died at the age of 96 on October 30, 1875, and his headstone—re-cut in 1939—is to be found in the churchyard at Thornton-le-Dale.

Two newspaper obituaries tells us that he served at first as a substitute in the Militia, then volunteered for active service, taking part in the last grand charge at Waterloo. He is described as "an old Peninsular soldier" and there is additional information that he served ten years in India in the 20th and 84th infantry regiments, and was at the taking of Seringapatam by General Baird. Referring to his time spent as Napoleon's guard, the newspaper account adds: "The old man used frequently to speak of having had the honour of shaking hands with the Emperor, and the recital evidently gave him great pleasure." He became an out-pensioner of Chelsea Hospital in 1830 and had been in receipt of 1s. $4\frac{1}{2}$d a day for 45 years.

Above: A Scandinavian longship is among the ironwork decorations on the 800-year-old south door of Stillingfleet Church.

Above: This rare "kneeling" cross, which may be between 600 and 800 years old, is on the north side of All Saints' church, Ripley.

*Above: The wild boar emblem of the Ingilby family
who have lived at Ripley Castle since the middle of
the fourteenth century, is to be seen above a
drinking fountain in the village's cobbled square.*

*Above: This simple headstone in the churchyard at
Thornton-le-Dale commemorates a local man who
was among Napoleon's escort on board the
Bellerophon during the voyage to St. Helena.*

TWO MONUMENTS

The approaches to Sledmere House, set on the northern rim of the Yorkshire Wolds, a quarter of a million acres of rolling country, are memorable for two remarkable monuments . . . a 60 ft cross in the style of those set up by Edward I for Queen Eleanor and the curiously carved stone drum of the Waggoners' Monument commemorating the 1,200 men who left their farms to join Sir Mark Sykes' company in the 1914—18 war.

The "Eleanor Cross", a copy of the Northampton monument, was designed by the architect Temple Moore in 1895 and convered in 1919 into a war memorial to the twenty-three local men who died. Their personal brasses attached to the monument have a medieval quality.

On the Waggoners' Monument the low-relief scenes are in deliberately naive style showing waggoners leading corn, enlisting, leaving their families, being kitted out, crossing the Channel and finally coming face to face with German troops.

Left: A Sledmere monument in the form of the Northampton Eleanor Cross commemorates the 23 local men who died in the 1914—18 war.

Right: The Waggoners' Monument at Sledmere is a reminder of the 1,200 men who left nearby farms to serve in the 1914—18 war.

TWO PALLADIAN TEMPLES

On the northern fringes of the Duncombe Park estate, near Helmsley, where the wooded land drops steeply towards the Rye valley and the sublime ruins of Rievaulx Abbey, a long, curving grass terrace commands one of the finest views in the county. At either end of this walk is a Palladian-style temple, added to the scene in about 1758, and between them creating a splendid example of large-scale landscape gardening in the Georgian era.

The temples—one rectangular and Ionic, the other circular and Tuscan—are now in the care of the National Trust. The architect is not known for certain, but it has been suggested that it was Sir Thomas Robinson, gentleman-architect friend of Lord Burlington, who built Rokeby Hall for himself and added the west wing to Castle Howard for his brother-in-law, the Earl of Carlisle. The Ionic temple is said to resemble one at Narford in Norfolk, which seems to be based on Palladio's reconstruction of a building in the Roman Forum. The pedimented portico has six tall pillars of York stone, and a plasterwork ceiling with echoes of Inigo Jones's work at the Whitehall Banqueting House. Inside, mythological scenes by Giuseppe Mattia Borgnis decorate the ceiling and cove. Motifs from the Palazzo Farnese in Rome (now the French Embassy) have been used. The carved woodwork is of exceptional quality.

The Italian plasterer Giuseppe Cortese, who was at work in Yorkshire in the mid-eighteenth century, may have had a hand in the decoration of the circular temple, where the inside of the dome has rich coffering. In the centre is a painted roundel of a winged god.

AN ASTRONOMER'S PYRAMID

Out of the rich grass of Sharow churchyard, near Ripon, rises one of Yorkshire's strangest tombstones. A perfect stone pyramid, it symbolises Charles Piazzi Smyth's pre-occupation with the Great Pyramid at Gizeh.

The long inscription is a tribute to his devoted wife Jessie who died in 1896 at the age of 80 and who was his "faithful and sympathetic friend and companion through 40 years of varied scientific experiments by land and sea, abroad as well as at home, at 12,000 feet up in the atmosphere on the windswept peak of Tenerife as well as underneath and upon the Great Pyramid of Egypt . . . "

Left: The rectangular, Ionic temple on the Rievaulx Terrace, near Helmsley. It is said to resemble one at Narford in Norfolk.

Right: The circular, Tuscan temple at Rievaulx. It dates, like its Ionic counterpart at the opposite end of the Terrace, from the mid-eighteenth century.

It was fitting that Smyth's middle name should commemorate the Sicilian astronomer, Giuseppe Piazzi, for the science of the skies was to enthrall him for a lifetime. When he died in 1900 aged 81 at his home at Clova, he was in the middle of a photographic study of cloud formations. But his life was overshadowed by a split between himself and the Royal Society whose members could not bring themselves to share his enthusiasm for the secrets of the Great Pyramid.

Born in Naples in 1819, the second son of a British admiral, he was educated at Bedford School and in 1835 joined the staff of the Royal Observatory at the Cape of Good Hope. The following year he saw Halley's great comet whose spectacular appearances about every 75 years have been recorded for more than 2,000 years.

When, in 1845, he succeeded Thomas Henderson as Astronomer Royal for Scotland, he found the observatory, established in 1818 on Calton Hill by the Astronomical Institute, to be in a sad state of repair. The Home Office showed no interest in its renovalion, though in 1896, eight years after Smyth had resigned the post in disgust at the continued reluctance to make improvements, the observatory was moved to its present site at Blackford Hill, Edinburgh.

The 25-pound gun which daily sends its one o'clock signal cracking across the Firth of Forth from the Half

Moon Battery of Edinburgh Castle is carrying on a tradition founded by Smyth, for it was in 1852 that he organised time-signalling by the dropping of a ball on Calton Hill. The time-gun took over in 1861.

In 1856 the Admiralty offered him £500 to be spent on experiments in telescopic vision from the peak of Tenerife. He travelled there in a borrowed yacht, the Titania. He published a popular account of his trip and embodied the results of the experiments in a paper for the Royal Society, who elected him a Fellow in June, 1857.

He spent the winter of 1864 in Egypt, measuring and surveying the Great Pyramid. In its proportions he found what he claimed was a cryptographic solution of the problem of squaring the circle, but a paper on the subject was denied a reading by the Royal Society, and he resigned his Fellowship. He retired to Clova where, in the clear air of the Ure valley, he turned his attention to the clouds.

A PRINCE'S MONUMENT?

The 800-year-old church of St. Helen and Holy Cross, which stands out on the eastern limb of the village of Sheriff Hutton with a view towards the Howardian Hills, has more to offer than quiet, box-pewed simplicity. It is believed by many to have something unmatched in any other parish church in the country . . .

an alabaster monument to a fifteenth-century Prince of Wales.

Faceless and with small hands folded in prayer, the figure on the monument against the church's north wall may represent Prince Edward, who died at Middleham Castle in 1484. He was the 11-year-old son of Richard III and his queen, Anne Neville, daughter of the Earl of Warwick. Until 1950 when it was re-assembled, the monument was split into four parts. Three slabs, including the figure, were on a window ledge, while the front panel rested against the wall. This was how it was seen by Capt. T. B. L. Churchill, who investigated the claims made on behalf of the monument in the early 1930's.

Although the passage of time must necessarily have left its scar on the monument, he said, it seemed probable that the alabaster had suffered, like so many other tombs of this material, from the belief that powder from scraping the stone provided a cure for diseases of the eye. The opinion has been expressed that the monument is undoubtedly Prince Edward's, but that the child was probably buried at Middleham

Right: Faceless and with hands folded in prayer, the figure on the alabaster monument against the north wall of the church of St. Helen and Holy Cross, Sheriff Hutton, is believed to be that of the 11-year-old son of Richard III.

where he died. The tomb, which had been made by the alabasterers of York, not being finished until after the death of Richard at Bosworth Field on August 22, 1485, may have been despatched to Middleham, but because of fear of Henry Tudor's men, was halted at Sheriff Hutton and erected there.

The York architect J. P. Pritchett, writing in the journal of the British Archaeological Association in 1887, had no doubt about the identity of the figure, and believed that the prince was actually buried in the church.

Further circumstantial evidence lies in the fact that as late as the end of the last century people in the area called the tomb "Little Crumplin", the inference being that here lay the "Little Crouchback" or the son of "Crouchback", the name given to Richard III by his Tudor detractors.

MEDIEVAL WALL PAINTINGS

One of the finest surviving galleries of mid-fifteenth-century wall paintings in the country dominates the interior of the parish church of St. Peter and St. Paul in Pickering.

After being discovered accidentally in 1851-52 they were covered up again until fully restored in 1878-79. A certain amount of damage was caused by the fixing and removal of memorial tablets. Perhaps the most striking of these murals, which are to be seen mostly on the north and south walls, are St. George and the Dragon and the martyrdom in AD 870 of St. Edmund, the 30-year-old last king of the East Angles, killed by invading Danes who fired arrows into his bound body. His shrine became the cathedral of Bury St. Edmunds in Suffolk.

Such decorations were common in the medieval church. The chronicler William of Malmesbury wrote: "We think it not enough . . . unless the walls glisten with various coloured paintings, and throw the reflection of the sun's rays upon the ceiling." In the time of Archbishop Ealdred (1061-69) the presbytery of the cathedral at York was adorned with a splendid representation of heaven.

Where wall paintings have survived into this century, they are often found under repeated coats of limewash and sometimes between work of earlier and later dates. The majority of the early paintings lasted 100 to 150 years before changing conditions and fashions obliterated them. But no matter how drastic the structural and decorative alterations, it was only very rarely that any attempt was made to erase the old work completely. At the Reformation in the sixteenth century many paintings disappeared for centuries, usually under limewash, the royal arms or scriptural texts. During the Gothic revival of the nineteenth century the restorers did a lot of harm by stripping away plaster to expose the building's outline.

TWO LIGHTHOUSES

One of England's noblest headlands—Flamborough—is the site of two lighthouses, one 300 years old and the other dating from 1806. The older lighthouse, an octagonal tower of chalk blocks from the high cliffs, was built in 1673-74 to the order of Sir Richard Clayton, and is said to be the oldest building of its kind in the North of England. It is still used as a landmark by Flamborough fishermen. A local man, George Mainprize, was at one time in charge of the light and had to keep an oak wood fire burning in the cresset on top of the tower. The fuel was stored in the base of the tower and the fire had to be stoked every three hours. In addition, Mainprize had to count the ships as they passed the headland.

The operational Trinity House light was built in the year following Trafalgar after the Bridlington Customs Collector had drawn attention to the large number of wrecks in the area. In the previous 36 years, 174 ships had gone down off Flamborough. The contract for the building went to John Matson of Prospect Street, Bridlington, who managed to work without the aid of external scaffolding. The lighthouse is 85 ft. high and is 250 ft. above sea level. Its brick tower was at first painted in bands of black and white, but it has been all white for many years now.

The older of Flamborough's two lighthouses was built in 1673-74 and is said to be the oldest building of its kind in the North of England.

Flamborough's operational lighthouse was built in the year following Trafalgar, and was the work of a Bridlington builder.

A CROMWELLIAN CHAPEL

Severely damaged in the gales of 1962 and restored in the autumn of 1966, the family chapel of 1649 in what were the grounds of the hall at Bramhope, between Leeds and Otley, is a rare example of a Cromwellian place of worship.

It was built to the orders of Robert Dyneley of Bramhope Hall. An ardent and unswerving Puritan, he left an endowment to provide "towards the maintenance of an able and godly minister."

Following the gale damage, which included the destruction of the small bell-cote, the chapel was in a sad state of decay. Well-established young trees blocked the door, and the interior was visible only through the mullioned windows with their individual arched lights. In places the ceiling was in danger of collapse, and a trimmed tree trunk had been inserted to support it.

The interior has a number of fine wall monuments, including one by Joseph Gott, a pupil of the York-born sculptor John Flaxman. The pulpit and some of the box pews had been removed and placed in a re-constructed, non-denominational setting in the Abbey House Museum at Kirkstall, Leeds.

The chapel came under the care of the former Wharfe-dale Rural District Council, who had acquired the building and the surrounding land by a deed of gift from the owner. They formed a Puritan Chapel sub-committee and got in touch with the Historic Buildings Council who, in turn, recommended to the then Ministry of Public Building and Works that a sub-stantial grant should be made towards its restoration. A local appeal was also successful.

The furnishings were returned from the Abbey House Museum to their original setting and the entire restor-ation of the building was carried out by craftsmen.

MEDIEVAL TILES

In the days when many a nobleman's hall had floors deep in straw and rushes, Byland Abbey, the Cistercians' largest English church, had a luxurious amenity . . . tiles of a green and yellow glaze set in geometrical patterns. Large areas of this tiling remain today in the two chapels of the south transept, though wear has revealed the red base in many places. Whitewash covered all the interior walls which were decorated with a masonry pattern in red. The carved capitals were also picked out in red. In the late fourteenth century wall paintings were added on the north wall of the north aisle of the nave, but these are no longer visible.

Right: Large areas of medieval tiling remain today in the two chapels of the south transept of Byland Abbey.

It was in 1177 that a much-travelled party of monks reached the site of today's ruins, not far from the village of Coxwold. Within 60 years they not only had their permanent home but drinking water, sanitation, properly drained arable land, a working mill- pond and well-stocked fish-ponds. They were undisturbed for more than 350 years until the Dissolution of the Monasteries destroyed their ordered life.

HOMECOMING OF LAURENCE STERNE

The bones of Laurence Sterne, novelist, lover, wit and dreamer, came home to Yorkshire in 1969, 201 years after his burial. near Tyburn, among executed criminals, in a plot infested by grave-robbers. His remains were reinterred with simple ceremony in the churchyard at Coxwold in North Yorkshire, the village where he held his last incumbency and lived comfortably in Shandy Hall.

He was the great-grandson of Richard Sterne, Archbishop of York in 1664-83 and nephew of Dr. Jacques Sterne, precentor and canon residentiary of York. About the time the first two volumes of his famous novel Tristram Shandy were printed and published in York, he moved to the Coxwold living. Up to this stage in his career (1759-60) he had been vicar of Sutton-on-the-Forest some miles to the south.

In 1967 the state of the rapidly deteriorating Shandy

Hall was considered by the Laurence Sterne Trust. Conditions were bad, as thirty years earlier an American literary researcher had commented on the building's need for renovation. In the February of that year I was invited to visit the hall by Mr. Kenneth Monkman, a devoted student of Sterne's life and work, who was to become the hon. curator. In Sterne's "best room" on the ground floor, the seventeenth-century panelling had survived, though the floor was almost completely decayed.

New life was injected into the house in the years following the Trust's 1967 appeal, so that Mr. Monkman, his wife and children, were able to move in. After six years' work the hall was drawn back from the brink of destruction. Sterne's "peaceful cottage" became a home once more.

The "best room" is now the dining-room and has a new oak floor. It was here that the main hall of the original medieval house stood, and behind the hinged white panelling of the small parlour is the painted wall of the old timber-framed house. During restoration, animal bones—probably those flung to the dogs from the dining table—were found under the rotted floor. An unmistakable survivor of medieval times is the huge chimney breast at one end of the house. In the seventeenth century a floor was inserted in the open hall, and two staircases were created in the same period. In the following century the house was gradually encased in brick.

The original kitchen of Shandy Hall's farmhouse days has the simple plate-rack and fireplace to be found in many cottages in the district. A wall oven from the famous Walker iron foundry in York (they made the railings outside the British Museum) carries the arms of Hanover.

Sterne was content in this Yorkshire retreat. "I am as happy as a prince," he wrote. "I sit down to venison, fish and wild fowl". Though there were times when he felt cut off, especially in winter.

He died in London shortly before four o'clock on March 18, 1768, in his first-floor lodgings with the wig-maker Mary Fourmantel in Old Bond Street, having gone to the capital to see into print the manuscript of A Sentimental Journey.

A YORKSHIRE NOVELIST

One of the country's largest Bronze Age standing stones is to be found in Rudston churchyard, on rising ground to the west of Bridlington. By contrast with this ancient gritstone memorial, the Romans who built a villa nearby were newcomers. The mosaic floors, including one of the quaintest portraits of Venus ever discovered, are now in the Hull Museum.

Right: In Rudston churchyard, on rising ground to the west of Bridlington, is one of the country's largest Bronze Age standing stones.

But there is more to draw the curious traveller. At the far edge of the churchyard, next to the burying place of the Macdonald of the Isles, is the open marble book which marks the grave of Winifred Holtby, who died in 1935 at the age of 37, just six months before the publication of her richly-textured regional novel, South Riding, which was dramatised for television in 1974.

Winifred Holtby was a farmer's daughter, born at Rudston on June 23, 1898. She became a successful journalist, author and political activist, campaigning for a variety of causes. Her first novel, Anderby Wold, was published in 1923 and was followed by five more books: The Crowded Street; The Land Of Green Ginger (a well-known street in Hull); Poor Caroline; Mandoa, Mandoa; and The Truth Is Not Sober. She began work on South Riding in March, 1934, renting a cottage at Hornsea, and the novel was published two years later. It was named Book of the Month and won the James Tait Black Memorial Prize for the best book of the year.

Yorkshire Television began filming the serialisation in the autumn of 1973 on the estuary below Welwick, on the road that eventually leads to Spurn Point. The White House, Winestead, appeared as "Maythorpe Hall", and then followed work at Hornsea, Pickering, Bridlington, Beverley and Holmpton.

The Winifred Holtby Society placed a memorial plaque in the church, but this remarkable woman is summed up by the inscription on the marble book outside . . . "God give me work till my life shall end, and life till my work is done."

MEDIEVAL PRIESTS

Tucked away in wold country not far from the main York to Bridlington road, Lowthorpe was probably a more than usually comfortable living for the priests and clerks who lived there in the fourteenth century. The church was made collegiate by Sir John de Hesellarton in 1333 at a time when the minister was so busy visiting the sick and carrying out his parish duties that there was no-one to celebrate daily services. It was found that profits were large enough "to support many persons" and six perpetual priests, with three clerks came to live in a manse which included a hall, chambers, kitchen, bakehouse, brewhouse and a loft. They had as much peat as they wanted and the priests had a clear annual stipend of six marks each. The clerks were paid 40s a year.

Two centuries later an inventory of church furniture included a silver chalice, two candlesticks, three bells

Right: Busy with priests in the fourteenth century, Lowthorpe church is tucked away in Wold country off the York-Bridlington road. Part of the church is now a roofless ruin.

in the steeple, four handbells and a sacring bell, a pair of old organs, two cruets, one old surplice, a suit of tawny worsted, a silk vestment with a yellow cross, a worsted vestment with a red cross, a silk cope "flowered with gold" and a black velvet suit slashed with gold.

Part of the church, which is charmingly sited on the edge of a patch of woodland and approached along an immaculate avenue of yews and flowering trees, is a roofless ruin, the shattered walls topped by birds' nests, the traceried windows blocked by ancient, rose-pink bricks. Close to the east end of the ruined chancel is a remarkable stone cross of a type uncommon in the neighbourhood and said to be the old market cross of nearby Kilham. Perhaps the most curious link with the past is the monument to be seen in the church itself—a man and woman carved on a grave slab and covered by a shroud. Between them runs the stem of a tree with branches appearing to grow across the bodies, each one ending in a child's head.

BURDALE TUNNEL

There is something unusual about the narrow cinder track which winds through the Wolds beyond Wharram-le-Street and past the site of an abandoned and excavated medieval village. Then round a bend in the road looms the entrance to Burdale Tunnel, a reminder that this is the route of the long-closed Malton-Driffield railway line. More than 120 years old and

1,734 yards long, the tunnel was blocked by a brick wall shortly after the line's closure to passengers on June 5, 1950, after a life of 97 years. It was closed to all traffic on October 20, 1958.

After seven years' work and a formidable array of obstacles, the opening trip took place in fine weather on May 19, 1853. The public attitude to railways is summed up in a comment on the opening published in the Yorkshire Gazette for May 21, 1853: "The time was when railways were looked upon by many as innovations to be deprecated and resisted—now they have come to be considered as ranking among the foremost blessings of modern civilisation."

The pleasures of rail travel were underlined by the Gazette's correspondent: "On both sides of the line, but especially to the south-west, the country has the appearance of a vast prairie, and when luxuriant crops wave their myriad heads in the autumn breeze the scene is rich in the extreme. The garden-like character of the soil, the neatness of the small, well-slashed fences, the immense numbers of sheep, the brisk and cheerful labourers, the substantial, well-situated farmhouses and beautiful undulating outlines of the country give a park-like appearance to the scenery, which is much heightened by innumerable plantations of fir which crown the heights and afford excellent shelter in winter."

Burdale Tunnel, which pierces a 300 ft ridge of the Wolds to reach, through chalk and shale, the Wharram Percy valley to the north, was described as being "by far the greatest railway work in the East and North Ridings." From the far side of the tunnel to Grimston the line was a succession of embankments, bridges and viaducts. "The very treacherous character of the clay has caused the most infinite trouble," said the Gazette. "Thousands upon thousands of tons of rock have been sunk to obtain secure foundations."

On the day of the opening trip, triumphal arches were erected, and lunch was provided by Lord Carlisle at Slingsby. The completion of this 19-mile stretch was coupled with the line from Malton to Thirsk, making a total of about 40 miles.

A RELIC OF NEWGATE PRISON

The underworld of Georgian London casts its shadow over a secluded corner of the richly-planted garden of Newby Hall on the north bank of the River Ure, near Ripon. A stone skull sits above a door which once led to a cell in Newgate Prison, the one from which Jack Sheppard, jail-breaker extraordinary, made his escape

Right: In a secluded corner of the garden at Newby Hall, near Ripon, is the door which once led to a cell in London's Newgate Prison from which Jack Sheppard made his escape in 1724.

one August day in 1724. As far as is known, the door was brought to Newby by Mr. Robert Vyner in the late-nineteenth or early-twentieth century.

Sheppard escaped no fewer than four times in 1724, and on Monday, August 30—the date recorded on the lintel of the door at Newby Hall—a warrant was sent to Newgate for the execution of Sheppard and other prisoners. His appointment with the hangman was postponed until the November after he had been betrayed and captured. Though armed with two pistols, he was too drunk to resist.

So over-confident was this petty thief that once, while on the run, he drove past the prison in a hackney coach with the blinds drawn. During his last brief days of freedom he dressed 'like a gentleman' in a black suit, tie-wig and ruffled shirt with a silver-hilted sword, diamond ring and gold watch. On the day set for his execution he was found to have an open knife in his pocket. He had planned to cut his bonds and throw himself out of the cart into what he hoped would be a sympathetic crowd, losing himself in the narrow alleys where the sheriff's officers could not follow on horseback. As a desperate measure he had also asked his friends to cut down his body, put it in a warm bed and open a vein.

A crowd estimated at 200,000 saw him hanged at Tyburn where his friends did indeed receive his body from the gallows and took it to a public house in Long Acre. In the evening he was buried in the churchyard of St. Martin-in-the-Fields.

A GEORGIAN THEATRE

The grey stone facade of Richmond's Georgian Theatre is off-set by its charming interior, once heated by open fires and lit by candelabra. Gas-lighting, first seen in London theatres in 1817, probably never reached this North Yorkshire playhouse.

The York actor-manager Samuel Butler built the theatre in Friars' Wynd, and it opened on September 2, 1788, with Earl Fitzwilliam, Sir Robert Dundas and Lord Pontefract among the audience. It was in regular use until 1830, but in the following 18 years performances became less frequent, and the building was let as an auction room. In time it was to become a corn chandler's store, a furniture repository and, in the 1939-45 war, a salvage depot. It was not until 1943 that a theatrical performance was staged to mark the enfranchisement of the town by the Earl of Richmond in 1093. After the war a trust was formed and the theatre was restored, opening to the public in 1962.

Dr. Richard Southern, who had been closely concerned with the work, wrote at the time: "A great difficulty was to restore the effect of the original lighting. It is certain that this must have been, by modern standards, almost astonishingly dim and mysterious, but the attempt has been made to reproduce the atmosphere of the original candles as faithfully as possible, so that visitors may at least have a chance of comparing the witchery of the eighteenth century with the comparative blaze of the twentieth."

The original green scheme of decoration was restored throughout the auditorium; paintings on ceiling and cornice were also restored. Green was the traditional colour for the interior of English theatres two centuries ago, and red for the canvas hangings lining the boxes. Traces of these hangings still survived in the Richmond theatre.

Theatre historian Ivor Brown, writing at the time of the theatre's re-opening, commented on the surprisingly small auditorium. Records of prices and takings suggested that as many as 400 patrons must have found room there. But Georgian play-goers were willing to suffer for art, and even the wealthiest members of the public accepted discomfort.

PATTERN OF POOL AND TEMPLE

Had it not been for the notorious eighteenth-century financial scandal known as the South Sea Bubble, which ruined many an English family, the superbly landscaped grounds adjoining Fountains Abbey might not have materialised, and the abbey itself could have become ivy-strangled and forlorn.

In low evening sunlight, when shadows stretch across the rich lawns, there are few lovelier spots in Britain than the Moon Ponds of the Studley Royal estate. On its sleek turf ramparts the Temple of Piety, backed by deep woodland, draws the sublime pattern into a whole, so that at times the ruined abbey appears to be the most stupendous garden "ornament" of all time.

John Aislabie was the man who saw the possible beauty of lake, canal, lawn and temple in the valley of the little River Skell which ran through the estate he inherited from an elder brother in 1699. He was also the Chancellor of the Exchequer implicated in the South Sea Bubble. After his release from the Tower, to which he had been committed on charges of "infamous foolhardihood and corruption", he withdrew to Studley Royal where all his energies were channelled into the improvement of the estate until his death in 1742.

It was about 1718 that Aislabie began to work on this magnificent landscape, and ten years later it was looked upon as the "wonder of the North." In the Travel Journal of Philip Yorke (1744) is recorded: "Imagine rocks covered with wood, sometimes perpendicularly steep and craggy, or others descending in slopes to beautiful lawns and parterres, water thrown into twenty different shapes."

Early stages of the work were in the hands of Aislabie's agent John Storaker whose accounts show that in August 1718 several labourers were paid for seventeen days' work at the canal. A Mr. Herve (perhaps the carver Daniel Harvey who settled at York and worked on Castle Howard) was paid £3 10s for two flower pots.

Aislabie's son William bought the abbey ruins from John Michael Messenger in 1768 and also took possession of Fountains Hall, built from abbey stone by Sir Stephen Procter about 1600. Unlike many eighteenth-century romantics, William liked his landscapes to be tidy, and he undoubtedly saved what was left of the abbey by clearing out the trees rooted in its walls.

A LONELY CHAPEL

Many of the 30,000 dead after the Battle of Towton, fought in a snowstorm on Palm Sunday, March 29, 1461, are said to have been buried close to the little manorial chapel of St. Mary which stands isolated in a field near the hamlet of Lead, a little way south of Tadcaster. A simple rectangle with bellcote and rustic pews, it probably dates from the early fourteenth

Left: Reflected in the Moon Ponds of the Studley Royal estate, the classical Temple of Piety stands on sleek turf ramparts backed by deep woodland.

century. In the early 1930's parties of hikers from the industrial West Riding began to use the chapel for services. They limewashed the interior and raised money to restore the glass. A service of re-dedication was held on November 6, 1932. Two years later the roof was removed and decayed timbers and slates replaced at a cost of about £80. New roof slates came from an old building at Scarthingwell Park near Saxton and from an old oil mill at Woodhouse Grange.

On a roadside site about a mile from the cottages and farms of Towton stands a stone cross—the battle memorial. It has been said that viewed on a percentage basis the casualties that day exceeded those of the Somme or the Marne. It was about 11 a.m. when the Yorkist army moved up from Saxton towards the present monument and the battle, which involved about 100,000 troops, began. There is a legend of a ring turned up centuries later by a ploughman. Perhaps the last gift from a girl to a Towton knight, it was inscribed: "En loial amour tout de mon coeur."

A WAYSIDE MAZE

Though the maze cut into the turf by the roadside near Dalby in North Yorkshire actually dates from the beginning of the twentieth century, it has ancient links with Scandinavia and the Danes who settled this tract of land. Its form was preserved through a carving which once existed on a barn door.

Taken over by the then North Riding County Council in 1930, it was said to be the only surviving instance in the area of an ancient game. Mazes pass under various names in different parts of England, such as Julian Bower, Robin Hood's Race, Shepherd's Ring, Walls Of Troy or City Of Troy, the last being the name by which this example has always been known. Similar mazes in Scandinavia are called Trojeborg (Troy Town). Reference to the game is found in Shakespeare's A Midsummer Night's Dream written in 1594.

Much uncertainty about the maze was removed some years ago when a member of the Scarborough and District Archaeological Society spent several days in the district interviewing old residents and drawing on oral tradition. He was told that the maze was cut on its present site in 1900, replacing an identical pattern made about 1860 which lay a little to the west and had been defaced by horses' hooves and farm wagons. A former roadman, living at Skewsby, and then 80 years old, said his grandfather recalled that the 1860 cutting had been copied from a carving on a barn door at Skewsby at a time when the Dalby maze could not be recognised on the ground. It seemed probable to the researcher that the door carving was the means of perpetuating the traditional design of a succession of ancient mazes, possibly originating in Viking times.

LONELY CIRCLE ON THE MOOR

Stonehenge has been tamed. For all its great age it is not quite the awe-inspiring experience it should be, standing on its neatly clipped and gravelled plot, sandwiched between two traffic-laden roads. The visitor need hardly step out of his car to get the message.

But if you are prepared to exchange antiquity for pure atmosphere then Yorkshire has something with far more visual impact. High up on the moors beyond four-square, stone-built Masham, is a Stonehenge-like circle built by the unemployed in the 1820's. True, it is a rich man's "folly", but visited on a summer evening as the shadows deepen in the surrounding woods, it is a spell-binding sight. Though much smaller in scale than Stonehenge—it measures 100 ft. by 50 ft. with some of the stones standing ten feet out of the ground—it compensates with the strength of its romantic appeal.

On the perimeter of the Forestry Commission plantation on which it stands are dotted other stone structures, lonely outriders of the main circle. Beyond them are superb views of remote reservoirs and the

Right: High on the moors, beyond Masham, is a Stonehenge-like circle built by the unemployed in the 1820's. It measures 100 ft by 50 ft with some of the stones standing 10 ft out of the ground.

hills rolling towards the Whernsides.

A CIVIL WAR BATTLE

In the quiet farmland five miles west of York a simple stone, roadside monument is the only reminder of a decisive battle fought in 1644 during the Civil War. To those who do not know the area, the name Marston Moor is a little misleading, for the battlefield in the mid-seventeenth century was open ground, broken up in the east part by shallow ditches and dotted with furze bushes.

The Parliamentarian-Royalist clash took place on July 2, three months after York was first surrounded by the besieging armies of the Earl of Leven, Lord Fairfax and the Earl of Manchester. In June the Parliamentarian armies made determined attacks on the city, capturing two Royalist gun batteries and erecting another of their own on a hill to the east. Much of the city's suburban area was burned, St. Mary's Tower on the corner of Bootham and St. Mary's Hamlet was blown up and there was an abortive attack on the King's Manor in the city centre. By the end of that month Prince Rupert with a Royalist relieving army reached Knaresborough, and the Parliamentarian armies raised the siege. The day before the battle the Parliamentarian armies were drawn up on Marston Moor expecting an attack from the west, but Prince Rupert outflanked them and approached from the opposite direction. Despite the prince's brilliant manoeuvres, the outcome was a Parliamentary victory, the siege was renewed on July 4 and twelve days later York surrendered.

The battlefield stretched between Tockwith in the west and Long Marston in the east, a distance of about two-and-a-quarter miles. Early in the day Cromwell received a light wound in the neck and it is said that he had it dressed in a cottage on the outskirts of Tockwith which was destroyed by a crashing aircraft in the 1939-45 war.

Some 4,300 dead were buried after the three-hour battle, the majority of them Royalists, in pits dug by the local people.

Among the wounded Royalists who finally reached the city was John Dolben, a young Oxford scholar who had joined the king's cause. While serving as an ensign and carrying the colours at Marston Moor he was wounded in the shoulder by a musket ball, and during the siege of York had his thigh broken. After the war he entered the church and in 1683, nearly 40 years after his experiences in the defeated throng at Micklegate Bar, he was enthroned sixty-seventh Archbishop of York. His reclining effigy is to be seen on a marble monument in the south choir aisle of York Minster.